BONFIRE SALOON

A NARRATIVE POETRY SNAPSHOT OF THE ALASKA GOLD RUSH, NOME, DECEMBER 3, 1903

STEVE LEVI
ARTWORK BY AMANDA SAXTON

PUBLICATION
CONSULTANTS
We Believe In The Power Of Authors

PO Box 221974 Anchorage, Alaska 99522-1974
books@publicationconsultants.com—www.publicationconsultants.com

ISBN Number: 978-1-63747104-3
eBook ISBN Number: 978-1-63747-105-0

Library of Congress Number: 2022936438

Photographs courtesy of the Alaska Digital Archives

Manufactured in the United States of America

Nome is on the westernmost tip of the Seward Peninsula, which juts out into the Bering Sea. The city is 735 air miles north of the Aleutian Islands, and every one of those miles is covered with a mantle of ice, ten feet thick from mid-September until early June. So in 1903, if you were not out of Nome by the end of September, you would be there until June. So this is what Nome looked like on every one of those days.

TABLE OF CONTENTS

ALASKA!

It is the land of the Alaska Gold Rush, where nuggets the size of goose eggs littered the ground, where men froze to death in search of the elusive yellow metal and dancehall girls lured overnight millionaires into marriage. Honky-tonk pianos punctuated the howl of the north wind in communities that were half tent and half ramshackle collections of driftwood, whalebone and packing cases.

It was a time of whiskey and gold and long, lonely trails behind a dogsled. In truth, the Alaska Gold Rush was all of that. It was a riotous time with saints and scoundrels living side-by-side. In the cities, rugged men and women walked on planks set across streets so deep with spring mud, horses could be swallowed whole.

From the four corners of the earth, tourists still come to the northland believing that as they walk the streets of Juneau, Nome and Fairbanks, they may very well hear the ghostly honky-tonk of the saloon pianos echoing across more than a century drawing them back to the wild and woolly days when the very word "Alaska" set the imagination of the world ablaze!

To fully appreciate the saga of the *Bonfire Saloon*, it is critical to understand the geography of the landscape. As you examine a map of Alaska you will see a string of 300 islands extending west from the mainland. This archipelago stretches for 1,200 miles, about the same distance as from Los Angeles to Austin, Texas, and extends so far west it becomes East. That is, the last island on the Aleutians is Attu, the site of the bloodiest battle during the Second World War. Attu is 6 degrees into the Eastern Hemisphere. Thus Alaska is the most northern, western and eastern of the states of the United States.

In a state of oddities, the Aleutians are an anomaly. The southern shore of the Aleutian Islands are swept by the Japanese Current, the *Kuroshio*. It is this current which keeps the North Pacific ice-free. But there is no complementary current on the northern shore of the Aleutian Islands. There the mantle of ice on the Bering Sea can be 15 feet thick and stops all marine traffic from mid-September to the beginning of June.

Every year!

Because the distance between the warm, southern shore of the Aleutians and the ice-cold northern waters of the Bering Sea are so close – in some cases zero feet – the Aleutians have the worst weather in the world. Warm air from the south mixes with frigid winds from the north making weather patterns that are not only unpredictable;

but deadly. As Alaskans say, in the Aleutians there are no atmospheric patterns: weather just arrives. The sky can be clear at 10 a.m. and be socked in at 10:05 a.m. And it can stay socked in for ten days.

Flying in the Aleutians is, under the best of conditions, treacherous. There are few places to land and like bear stories, every Alaskan who has flown in the Aleutians has a tale to make you want to stay in the big city. In Cold Bay, for instance, it is not unusual for a bush plane to crab to port on takeoff and then, midway down the runway, crab to starboard because there are two, 50-mile-an-hour winds blowing 180 degrees from each other with the winds interfacing halfway down the runway. "Every time I think I about flying in the Aleutians," is a favorite bush pilot expression, "I don't." As Alaskan humorist Warren Sitka notes, "In Alaska, wild animals, children and weather in the Aleutians are predictably unpredictable."

Why is this important to understand the events in the *Bonfire Saloon*? Because

Nome, 143 miles south of the Arctic Circle, is 736 air miles north of the Aleutians.

Across the Bering Sea.

Which freezes with a mantle of ice 15 feet thick.

Today, and during the Alaska Gold Rush, the last ship to leave Nome had/s to be out of the Bering Sea by about September 15th. After that, no ship can make it into Nome until the next June. During the Gold Rush, if you were in Nome on September 16th, you were there until June. And you'd better have the money to make it through the winter. In Nome, during the Gold Rush, just before that last steamship of the season left, all of the derelicts, homeless and destitute were rounded up and put onboard an outgoing steamer. This was called 'getting a Blue Ticket' because the color of the Alaska Steamship Company tickets was blue.

The Nome Rush was unusual for three reasons. First, you could arrive by steamship. To get to Nome, all you had to do was buy a ticket. There was no hiking involved. Because the Nome harbor was so shallow, the argonauts had to be lightered ashore. In the background of this photograph of a cargo barge coming ashore, you can see the sailing ships anchored offshore.

Second, while there were mines well back from the city, the bulk of the argonauts were on the beach. The beach was federal property so you could not stake a claim. But you could dig for gold on the sandy beach.

When the tide was low.

So, every 12 hours from June to September, like an army of ants, gold seekers swarmed onto the beaches with pots, pans, cradles along with a wide range of gold extraction contraptions and separated the gold nuggets and flakes from tons of sand. But only from the sand where you were standing, an area which extended on all sides as far as your shovel could reach.

Third, everything Nome needed had to come in by ship: food, clothing, whiskey, medical supplies, horses, mules, tables, chairs, pipes, stools, bar counters, et cetera. Further, Nome had no nearby forest so all wood for homes and coal for heat had to come in by ship. This photo is of 10,000 tons of coal in burlap sacks to take Nome through the winter of 1902.

For those who enjoy trivia, many residents and gold seekers in Nome would shape American history. Wyatt Earp was in Nome but left in 1901, two years before the events in *Bonfire Saloon.* His combination saloon and brothel, Dexter, can be seen on the left-hand side of the street in the following photo.

James "Jimmy" Doolittle, later of *Thirty Seconds Over Tokyo* fame, spent his early years in Nome – and earned a reputation as a boxer. Billy Mitchell, later to be court-martialed for browbeating the United States Navy to spend on airplanes rather than battleships, spent four years in Alaska stretching the telegraph wire that would connect Nome with the lower 45 states at that time. Of historical interest, on June 28, 1917, Mitchell was the first American pilot to fly a combat mission over Germany in what was then the Army Air Corps.

General James Doolittle	Brigadier General William L. Mitchell, United States Army Air Service

Then there was Wilson Mizner, a loveable scoundrel. Mizner was involved with gambling and prize fighting in Nome and it was said he was probably the only man with the reputation of being able to "borrow money from a lamppost and is said to be the onlly man who ever hired the Nome brass band on credit." In addition to these northern distinctions, in the course of Mizner's life he was also a mining engineer, actor, playwright, a Fifth Avenue art dealer, husband of the "second richest woman in the world," proprietor of the legendary Brown Derby in Los Angeles and, with his brother Addison, a founder and promoter of Boca Raton, Florida.

In Nome, Mizer was known as the Yellow Kid. He earned this sobriquet by putting syrup in his hair when he worked as a bartender. In those days whiskey was bought with gold dust. Mizner's fingers, sticky from the syrup in his hair, would pick up few grains of gold dust every time he weighed out gold dust for a drink. He would occasionally run his fingers through his hair thus transferring those gold dust grains onto the strands of his hair. After his shift, he would shampoo his hair and pan for the flakes. This scam, true, is included in "Whiskey Jack."

In 1902, Mizner was involved in a badger game in which he was to play the "damaged husband." He drank too heavily the night before and when he awoke, late for his appointment to break in on the love birds, he discovered his pistol had been stolen. Looking for a prop, he found a can of tomatoes and stripped off its label. Thus armed he crashed into the lover's nest and threatened to blow up the two lovers. The man paid for his life with his money belt which yielded $10,000 in gold. After the man had fled in terror, Mizner's partner asked for her share of the boodle. Mizner handed her the tomato can. When she asked what good the can was going to do her, Mizner calmly stated, "It just got me $10,000." This con is included in *Jimmy the Goat*.

True, as well was the theft of $40,000 from the Gold Commissioner's office in Dawson in *Marshal Jew Bob*. Depending on the source, the thieves were either Scurvy Bill and Two

Tooth Mike, or Mit, Half-Kid and Two-Tooth Mike. Mizner listed himself as the Deputy Sheriff at the time but he probably meant Deputy United States Marshal. By his own admission, just after Mizner had hidden Scurvy Bill in his own attic, Mizner was called to join a posse in looking for the very criminal he had just hidden. The posse followed a blood trail to a cabin where it was assumed the criminals were hiding. Mizner astonished the posse by "rolling a cigarette in one hand and holding a revolver in the other" and then kicking in the log cabin door. History does not record what happened to the bank robbers – or, for that matter, what happened to the $40,000. Additionally, possibly true, according to Mizner, he once robbed a restaurant in Nome for chocolates for his girlfriend *Nellie the Pig* with the words, "Your chocolates or life" and grubstaked the future owner of Grauman's Chinese Theater in Los Angeles.

At the time of the events in the *Bonfire Saloon*, Nome had a population of about 15,000 people and stretched ten blocks deep along 20 miles of the Bering Sea coast. At the southern end of the Nome strike was Solomon which had a railroad. The locomotive and cars – originally owned by New York City – had been transported to Nome in 1903, the year of the *Bonfire Saloon*. A huge storm washed out the rails in 1913 and the train was left where it was. It can still be seen today – both physically and virtually – as "The Last Train to Nowhere."

This is a not a book of narrative poetry. It is a book of history disguised as literature. The slang, words, terms and expressions in the narrative are those which would have been used in the saloon in 1903. I found as many relevant photographs of Nome in 1903 as I could and left all identifying script on the photographs. None were photoshopped and I chose the most expressive snapshots even if they were not of the highest resolution. This work is designed to drag you, kicking and screaming, back more than a century, and bowl you over with a street level snapshot of people and events which did or could reasonably have occurred in Nome at the height of the Alaska Gold Rush. The line drawing of Peg Legged is actually that of Captain Charles Lewis, Captain of Alaska's Ghost Ship, the *Clara Nevada* from a Peruvian legal monograph, an example of how far the tentacles of the Alaska Gold Rush reached.

During the Alaska Gold Rush, when the Yukon and Kuskokwim rivers and the Bering Sea froze over, you were there until June. You would be living in a small cabin with the people who chose to stay, not those you chose to stay with. Individuals who had difficulty adjusting to their cabin mates and went stir-crazy were said to have "cabin fever." As winter approached, you chose your friends carefully, but once the rivers froze, you'd be cooped up with them for nine months.

Actual Names of Alaska Gold Rush Argonauts

Many of the argonauts, good time girls and cons in Nome had reasons *not being* in the lower states. They could not use their real names in Alaska. So they did not. And the practice spread across the District. (Alaska did not become a Territory until 1912 and did not become a State until 1959.)

All of the names in this book are authentic. The following list of sobriquets are actual individuals whose *activities* have been lost to history

MEN

Waterfront Brown	Swiftwater Bill	Billy the Turk
Step and a half	Two Step Louie	Buckskin Harry
Eat-em-up Frank	Hard Luck Charlie	Muck-Luck Kid
Scurvy Kid	Skylight Kid	In and Out Kid

Malamoot Kid	The Dutch Kid	The Daylight Kid
Dago Kid	Blueberry Kid	Forty-mile Kid
Sixty-Mile Kid	The Crummy Kid	Honest Ike
Deep Hole Johnson	Too Much Johnson	Husky Kid
Slivers Perry	Slivers Feiges	Powerful Joe
Blackie	Squeaky Pete	Hot Air Smith
Brainey Smith	Windy Smith	Jumping Smith
Happy Jack	French Joe	Cock-eyed Shorty
John the Greek	Moose John	Butch Stock
Ham Grease Jimmy	Hungry Mike	Poker Charlie
Montana Pete	Blueberry Tommy	Dago Joe
Two for a Quart	Mush-on	Snuff Box Olsen
Snowy	Jimmy the Goat	Wise Mike
Komoko John	Long Shorty	Stone-age Bill
Tanglefoot	Three-Fingered Bob	Dog Sam
The Black Prince	The Gambler's Ghost	The Coat
The Vest	Tripod Pete	Diamond Dick
Jimmy the Goat	Sawdust King	Gypsy Joe
Coon Skin Bill	Handsome Harry	Popcorn Jimmie
Tommy the Skunk	Possible Straight Kid	Ring Tail Squealer
Charles the Twelfth	Dead Eye Dick	Twelve to Two
Chili Dick	Pete the Pig	Three Fingered Bob
One Armed Jake	Hokey Pokey White	Jimmie Craps
Fatty Bill	Fifteen to Two	Tommy the Rat
Peg Legged Jack	Baked Bean Leo	Punctual Carp

Swiveled Eye Kid	Buzzard Kid	Slaughterhouse Mike
Rotten Egg Mike	Kangaroo Jack	Shanghai Huber
Roulette Joe	Economic Willie	Leo the Nonpareil
Socialist Kid	Hatless Joe	Little Giant
Whisky Jack	Claw Hammer Bill	Cheese ham Sam
Scotch Albert	Turnip Mike	Gee Pole Johnson
Keyhole Jimmy	Dirty Pete	Bar
Forty Horse Power Swede	Muck Luck Kid	Dogface Johnny
St. Peter of Tanana	Penny Ante Brown	High-grade Sweeney
Stampede Bill	Ground sluice Bill	Itchy Scratchy
Laughing Ole	Crummy Kid	Marshal Jew Bob
Pete the Pig	Phonograph Nelson	Pistol-grip Jim
Crooked-Neck Jorgenson	Squeaky Pete	

WOMEN

The Nosey Sisters	The Virgin	Passionate Annie
The Limping Grouse	Bunch Grass	The Oregon Mare
The Utah Filly	The Black Bear	The Cub
Spanish Marie	Spanish Julia	Finn Annie
Snow Ball	Spot	Moose Mary
Short and Dirty	Dirty Gertie	Queenie
Three-Way Annie	Web Foot	Diamond Tooth Gertie
Diamond Hattie	Skagway Kay	May the Cow
Allah, Allah, Allah	Kitty the Bitch	The World's Wonder

The Merry Widow	Cheechako Lil	The Chinless Wonder
French Camille	Nellie the Pig	Sweet Marie
The Sweet Pea Girl	Maggie the Rag	Moosehide Annie
Laughing Annie	Irish May	Texas Rose
Butter Ball	The School Marm	Fighting Nell
Fuzzy Knot	Box Car Aggie	The Dough-nut Queen
Sixty-Nine	Connie the Wiggler	Brown Gravy
Doghouse Lezzy	White Rat	Jew Rose
Piled River Maud	Limping Grouse	Pissing Jenny
Spitting Maud	Incan Anne	Dago Marie
Pig-Faced Patsy	Louise Dick	

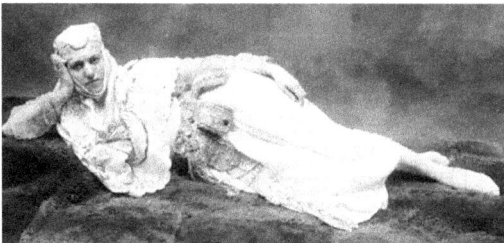

HARRISON HILL COMIC TRAVELING TROUPE

In the dawn of the day of the searching for gold
when men with their sluices and hope in their soul
scattered along the Bering Sea shore
scratching the sand for the color of ore,
a troupe of performers from Harrison Hill,
North Carolina, were packing a still.

The Alaska Gold Rush made an offer rare
for the poor of the nation to become millionaires.
All they had to do was flood to the north
then, with shovels and pans, prove your own worth
by plunging their shovels into the earth
and dividing the nuggets of gold from the dirt.

The Harrison Hill Comic Traveling Troupe
found the best way its upfront costs to recoup.
Rather than earning wealth by pebble and flake
they schemed to mine sourdoughs' pockets to take
nuggets and flakes, cash and doubloons
selling floorshows and whiskey in a first-class saloon.

Nome had been chosen for the most obvious reason:
it was well known it had double seasons.
The first began when the ice mantle broke
on the Bering Sea's chest and proceeded to soak
the shore from the Aleutians and then to the west
to the rugged coastline of Siberia's chest.

In the late fall came the annual crush
when the Bering Sea waters were reduced to a slush
and thereafter to ice measuring fifteen feet thick
with *polynyas*, blizzards and lost lunatics,
leaving the land frozen in place
from ides of September until the next May.

As barons of booze they knew that the gold
would only be found by a few of the souls
who were feeding their dreams on suet and beans
for the sparkle of nuggets in cold mountain streams
and the greatest of profit to be wrung from this throng
would come from the sale of whiskey and song.

So the troupe gambled these men of the earth
would be willing to pay for an evening of mirth –
coupled, of course, with the juice of the still
made from the leavings of fruit from the hill:
berries and currents and rose hips in stew
mixed together with sugar and yeast in a brew

known as Honeypot Whiskey, the liquor was sold
with a front row seat ticket for a nugget of gold
weighing an ounce when the cover of snow
was as deep as axe handles – four set head-to-toe –
when the diggings were frozen solid 'till spring
and the miners were free to drink whiskey and sing.

One of the blessing of Nome, be it said,
was the issue of tickets of blue to the dead
drunks of the town and those with no means
to make 'til springtime without any green
on the backs of the sheets of paper called cash
off to Seattle they were shipped out like trash.

Thus there only remained, latched tight in the snow,
were men who had cash with eight months to blow,
for mining by pan, sluice and pushcart
was stalled 'til Bering Sea ice did depart
in the middle of June when the barges came in
with a fresh batch of patrons ready for gin.

In the summertime sun when mosquitoes came out
and the daylight grows longer and fiddleheads stout,
the troupe and their gear could head into the bush
where miners would gather when the end of the slush
meant standing in water both knee-deep and cold
and an evening of laughter was worth nuggets of gold.

This offered the Harrison Hill Comic Traveling Troupe
two business seasons their upfront costs to recoup,
winter in town and summer on trail,
the saloon set on Front Street and a smaller scale
of women and sets and Honeypot Whiskey
to harvest the mobs of sourdoughs frisky.

In town, the troupe owned the Bonfire Saloon
offering whiskey and doughnuts, starting at noon
until the next noon and thereafter each day
the same diet and drink 'til Judgement Day
and special floor shows every evening at six
with scantily dressed sweeties as part of the mix.

The curtains would rise and a man in a vest –
complete with a medal for mirth on his chest –
warmed up the crowd with his off-color jokes
of blackies who choked on squaw candy pokes,
of women of silk and satin and lace
in leather with whips and rouge on their face.

Then the women in leather and dresses of lace
would wade through the crowd with courage and grace,
raking in nuggets the size of a goose eggs
and all the gold dust the women could peg
was tied up in pokes of rawhide and string
and stored in a locker 'til the coming of spring.

To increase their percentage, the troubadours found,
was simply a matter of tilling new ground
or, in this case, in this land of wild dreams
was the import of water from cold mountain streams
used at a ratio of seven to three:
the seven for water, the rest for whiskey.

The miners kept coming, by packs and by pairs,
plugging the floor from the stage to the stairs
tossing nuggets on stage in a sweet golden rain,
mineral gifts from Alaska's terrain,
which the damsels scooped up from off the dance floor
and not one of them said, "Please, throw no more."

On the 9th of December in Nineteen Ought Three
when ice covered the chest of the Bering Sea,
the Bonfire Saloon hosted an evening of ale
along with bare bellies, thighs and pigtails,
a routine to lure miners to spend on their dreams
with gold nuggets secured from Snake River streams.

Moose Ptarmigan Ben and Rabbit Nose Bob
stood shoulder-to-shoulder in the swirl of the mob
on the snow-slickened floor of the Bonfire Saloon
drinking the swill and sidestepping spittoons
with Peg Legged Jack and Economic Willie,
Marshal Jew Bob and Claw Hammer Billie.

Present as well was Cheechako Lil
and her bed-friend of the moment, Caribou Bill.
Against the back wall beside Cast Iron Kid
was Charles the Twelfth with his tobacco chew lid
and Rotten Egg Mike and Kangaroo Jack
standing shoulder to shoulder with Tommy the Rat.

The doors never closed at the Bonfire Saloon
and the price of the hooch was as high as the moon;
the best could be bought with a handful of flakes
be it pork roast or thigh or fresh Johnny-cake;
a break from the darkness of days upon end
when a panful of beans was your best friend.

Buzzard Kid

The Buzzard Kid's one to despise.
To be nice he never tries.
He steals other's whiskey
and when he feels frisky,
takes coins from a dead man's eyes.

Moose Ptarmigan Ben

Moose Ptarmigan Ben had been drinking since noon
on September 15th . Until the next June
his claim on both shorelines of Churnagain Creek
would be snow-locked for winter. With his paystreak
he would seek succor in this ice-prison maroon
with Honeypot Whiskey in the Bonfire Saloon.

A sourdough tall with flakes from his claim,
he was paying top dollar to see traveling dames,
not Kitty the Bitch or Maggie the Rag,
the local trollops who were paid by the bag
in beds or on tables or upstairs or on floors
well-known in the Bonfire as resident whores.

Moose Ptarmigan Ben wanted a wife
who'd share his good fortune for the rest of his life.
He was doin' quite well on Churnagain Creek
living nose-to-nose and turning his cheek
to those whose gold pans were churning up grey
gravel and stones and roots in decay.

Moose had failed in all he had done,
since the day of his day of birth in the Florida sun.
His orange trees had died on the vine
and boll weevils on his cotton had dined.
He had punched cattle and they had punched back
leaving him with a most painful back.

He took a turn with a badge and a gun
which gave him the cash to pull up stakes and run
North where money came in a different form
and offered him the chance to transform
from a man who'd never turned a good card
but was willing for wealth to work quite hard.

When asked by the others why he joined the rush
Moose pulled his hat low and then quickly cussed
that he was just like most other men
who had not to wealth a connection
so like a frog on lily pads he did leap
when the water of failure rose on his feet.

Like the very few in the north
he could not afford to trust his whole worth,
and his claim and his beans and cabin lot
to the mercy of the neighboring sots
who spent their winter frozen in
and survived on baked beans and rotgut gin.

So he locked himself onto his claim
from freeze-up 'til the springtime came
and with a shotgun chaperoned
his sixty feet of frozen loam.
But allowed himself a few doubloons
for an infrequent night in the Bonfire Saloon.

It wasn't that Moose was adverse to sex
or was a monk when it came to the mix
of male and female on the occasional whim
rather, he had understood that he with him
his road in life had a ways to go
and that way did not include grit and the snow.

Yes, he would drink in the Bonfire Saloon.
But, no, he would not howl at the moon
until his pouch was as flat as a tide-swept beach
after a storm and tide had its reach.
He had only two cares while he was in town,
two problems to solve while he was ice-bound.

First were his flakes from deep in the soil,
the bounty of his time, sweat and moil.
For those flakes to make it from claim to town,
he had to make sure he wasn't shot down.
Then came the conversion from flakes to doré
by a honest man who did the assay.

The finding of gold is child's play to most.
If it's there you'll find it but if you boast
you're loaded with ingots to the wrong folks
you'll end up with buckshot if not plain broke
so you husband your findings protecting your nut
and most important, keep your mouth shut.

That was the first step in his passage to wealth
and there still remained one other of stealth.
Pancakes of gold in Nome cannot buy
farmland in Kansas and clothes in July
if the sum of the gold cannot leave Nome
and in lower states find a safe home.

The ongoing labors of Marshal Jew Bob
was keeping gold safe from those who would rob
be it intown where no gaming was fair,
(conmen with marked cards and false millionaires)
or on the mud road into Nome under the stare
of road agents with shotguns or a winter bear.

Next came the step of converting doré
into documentation which would find its way
to banking branches in cities and towns
far to the south that were never icebound.
He needed a bank with a rock-solid link
to a rock-solid payee not on the brink

of losing it all by a run on the bank.
So through the crowd of keen mountebanks
he started his search for that man of repute
who had the credentials none would dispute.
That man was known as Kangaroo Jack
whose Australian bank was always in black.

Fortunes are products of luck, sweat and grit
and the gods favor those who will never quit,
but along with good fortune comes bugaboo
making the most alluring daydream come true
and it is easy to become to pleasure a slave
but to be successful, it's the money you save.

The Alaska Gold Rush was a multicultural event. Men – and quite a few women – rushed north from all over the world. These people only had one thing in common: gold.

Kitty the Bitch

You bastards with dicks know you've got it made,
live in the sunshine and leave us in the shade.
You can get jobs, earn cash for your worth,
while our only task is to give birth
to the increase in number of males in the brood
while the girls are viewed only as consumers of food.

Yeah, I'm a bitch, it's my middle name,
but it's more than a label, it's my passage to fame.
Yes, I make money flat on my back
but I'm more than a whore with my breasts stacked.
I'm a hoarder of nuggets, doré and flakes
and back to Seattle those items I'll take.

I know what I speak because I was the bitch
of my father and uncle and other male kith
from the time I turned ten in a Missouri town
where men started drinking when the sun went down
on their tenth birthday. Women were bound
to be nothing but chattel to be passed around.

I was sold to a steamboat – who said slavery was dead? –
as a whore for the crew, black, white and red.
When we arrived at the end of the trip
I was again sold, this time to a ship
of sailors who were going in search of the whale
in the farthest north waters. When under sail

I was shuttled about like a bird in a cage
servicing those regardless of age.
From the captain's bed at the bow of the ship
to the black whalers' bunks, trip after trip,
from Orleans to Cuba and rounding Cape Horn
we headed north and then west regardless of storms.

Off the coast of Hawaii I was swapped once more
for a girl half my age. I am sure the crew swore
I had been good for them but what they wanted was new
so a swap seemed the best thing for both ships to do.
Before I could jump ship and swim to the shore
I was locked in the hold to serve again as a whore.

I had but one chance and that was to run
or I'd swim with the fish after all men had their fun.
I had to be gone in the blink of an eye
overboard before any of the sailors were wise.
One night a leaking long boat was trailing
So I slipped up on deck and went over the railing.

I will not lie. I was taking a chance
for I know not where I was – but a glance
to the east I could see a shoreline
and I quietly paddled while lying supine.
Once on the shore I ran as fast as I could
concealing myself behind trees in the woods.

Did the crew ever come looking? I'll never know.
I just kept running faster away from the coast,
away from my past, the crew and the boat
with no shoes or trousers and no overcoat.
For three days I stumbled cold and afraid
naked and barefoot alone in the rain.

Does God have a plan? I'm not a believer
but strange things happen and I was delivered
into a huddle of *barabaras*
at the moment my fate was not assured of.
I was treated better by people in skins
then I ever was among my own kin.

Life in the Arctic is brutal at best
and the will to survive can never rest
for food from the land comes only in seasons
and thus there is every reason
to fillet all salmon and jerky all moose
for Old Man Winter offers no truce.

Then in the year of Nineteen Ought Two
news of a gold rush came in by canoe.
A new city was stretching on the sand like a snake
and there was a chance many dollars to make,
cash to supplant the salmon and moose
though it was putting my head back in a noose

for the leap between river and city life
was as broad as that from virgin to wife
but the promise of the money lures every man
and with them came wives and then the whole band.
Suddenly I was back in the clutches of men
but wiser this time then before I had been.

I'm Kitty the Bitch, but I have a plan
to never again be dependent on man
and my route to that goal is to gather my gold
and for the first time be paid for my soul
and when I have earned enough to live well
I'll steamship south and disappear into the hell
l

of the lower states where women are slaves
to the whim of a man and the lust that he craves.
The girls on the floor of the Bonfire Saloon
are saving no nuggets for the end of the boom.
They will die as they lived, with their backs on the floor
eking out that last trick in work they abhor.

No one has a choice from whence they began
and one can regret the roadways they ran;
we all make poor choices during our life
and no one's path forward is lacking in strife
but it's where you choose to finish your run,
not where you were forced to begun."

Nome does not have a forest. This meant the Natives of the region had to build their homes out of sod. Chunks of the sod would be cut from the soil and stacked to form barabaras.

CHARLES THE TWELFTH

Charles the Twelfth was nobody's fool,
the perfect man who would not be a tool
of the rich and well-placed, even in Nome,
and though he was seated far from his home
and regardless where he ate his meat and his bread
the Constitution was never lost in his head.

He was the right man in the right place
where his rulings solidified both fief and case
for there was only one man who could say "No,"
and he was the judge sent from Juneau.
So, for all along the Bering Sea coast
Charles was judge: cry or boast.

He had two agents which sealed his hold
on who owned what, both land and gold.
First was the ice 15-feet thick
which precluded escape from Nome by ship
from late September to the ides of June
and to flee inland was death for buffoons.

Second was the sing and song of wire,
telegraph, that is, and with courts it conspires
to trace miscreants where're they chose to hide
in village, towns or remote countryside,
for the arm of John Law feared no ice packs
so you keep your nose clean or you will be sent back.

To his annoyance were the niddle-noodles
who prattled on and on with flamdoodle
each with (perhaps) a legal quiddity
which could be quickly edited. He
always stood tall for the United States
in all matters: marriage, gold and estates.

But then again, he was no fool,
and if perchance he was asked to rule
on a matter which was poorly chosen
or because the land 'til June was frozen.
If you pulled a prank to 'jerk his chain'
he was one who could return the same.

Once whiskey was seized by a purblind priest
as proof of the local whiskey beast
and claimed all liquor in the north
was illegal. So the priest, to prove his worth,
wanted Charles to close the town to booze
and let Christian goodness thereafter ooze

through the saloons along Front Street
and waterfront to the tundra peat.
Charles looked at the law then over his glasses –
knowing there are fewer horses than asses
but asses bray and, at the very least,
the complaint had been lodged by a priest –

but this did not mean Charles could ignore
his duties as Commissioner.
So he called a jury of eleven men,
and to be fair, plus a woman,
Cheechako Lil who understood the want
of whiskey in her restaurant.

He gave the twelve the case to consider
and asked the matter be wrapped up by dinner.
The case, in this case, was both writ and booze,
the latter for the twelve to choose
if it was, indeed, violation of the law
or perhaps a liquid fraud.

So, the case, in this case, was passed about the room
for each a nip of the liquid to consume.
"Hoity Toity!" was the universal claim
that the case of whiskey in question, became
"lost in transit" was the legal term used
and recorded in the Commissioner's view

and as there was no chattel of prejudice
the case before the bar was dismissed.
Be it a game of skin, bosh or blunder
the Commissioner was the thunder,
the bolt of lightning over town
for it was he who kept the crime rate down

There was one place he let his hair down –
odd as there was no hair on his crown –
in the press of the Bonfire Saloon
where he was rubbed elbows with buffoons,
saints and sinners, goliaths and gnomes
and all in the north who called Nome home.

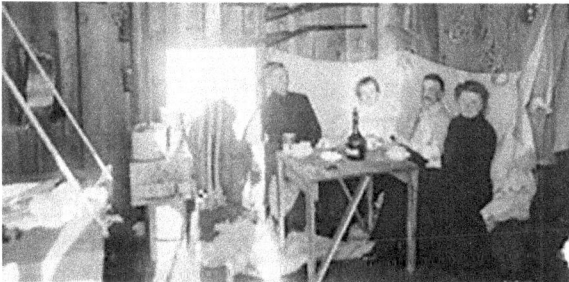

Windy Smith

Windy Smith was the man with the key
and fingers to match because he
was the man of the hour, nay, every hour
but it sunshine or windy, or in rain shower
for it was his desk in a driftwood shack
who monitored the telegraph's clack.

The Post Office was king 'tween June and September
for it brought more than the mail from those remembered
who had been abandoned or left widows of grass
who were best forgotten 'til the limitation had passed
but the steamboats brought
something to scare the escapers:
weekly bundles of US newspapers.

But after the last of the steamships fled south
Windy was all that was left of speech by mouth
and all other correspondence was over wire
and all business and news and legislative conspires
came over land with a clickety clack
and would wait for an answer to wind its way back.

This all be said Windy had an odd job
which he performed with Marshal Jew Bob.
There were those in Nome whose noses were clean
but not in the states where they were last seen
so it could be said that many a telegram got lost
in the trash and the mud and the green tundra moss.

CONNIE THE WIGGLER

Connie the Wiggler
wasn't a singer
or even a star of the stage
but covered with soap
she gave clients hope
their clothing would be quite the rage.

A laundress by trade,
but it silk or brocade,
her work was beyond repute
and there wasn't a man,
white, brown or tan,
who did not owe her salute.

She was well known
all over Nome –
if you prized your outer wear –
she'd cleanse your pants clean
from seam to seam
and repair it if there was a tear.

For women's bustles
she repaired ever rustle
and replaced every crack in whale bone
so you always sat pretty
on barstool or privy,
plank benches or campfire stones.

Be they blood stains
or bean dripping remains
Connie could wash color away
and return your vestments
without wrinkles or rents
in less than a handful of days.

There was always room
in the Bonfire Saloon
for everyone wished Connie the best
and she never searched
for a chair or a perch
for all the men wanted clean vests.

That being said,
Connie would see red
and refuse to wash certain shirts:
those with wrinkles in sleeves
for cards to receive
to appear in a manner expert

when a spreading of royals
would not be spoiled
by the quick insert of a King
or a handload of trash
could be converted to cash
by the deft flick of a finger ring.

Connie was clean
as Evangeline
even though she had wash board hands
but somewhere she knew
was a suitor in blue,
a patiently waiting man

who would sweep her away
some bright sunny day
and wash the Nome memories away
and that dream she would keep
with her elbows sunk deep
in the suds of her laundering ways.

DAGO JOE

Dago Joe was an Eskimo,
not really, just named so,
because he was the man with sled and dogs
who mounted with boots and togs
and ran the mail hither to and yon
in winter when there was no dawn.

His circuit, as the P. O. stated,
was village and town, open or gated,
be it 'skimo, white or Baptist,
Quaker, Catholic or polygamist,
for, just as in the lower states,
news is welcome even when late.

Ten percent of every village and farm
needs the reach of the P.O.'s arm,
for those who read were not just white
but full and half breed, troglodyte,
who lived in sin with stinking air,
in *barabara* or cabin square.

It was said by those with no grace
Dago Joe dragged to town a trace
of the bush as he often smelled of fish,
seal oil, walrus and some 'skimo dish
and the poop of dogs in teams,
along with sweat, grime and kerosene.

Once all of this has been said
those who need no news are dead,
for all the rest lack of news gives one fits
and leaves one with a constant itch,
to know what's been goin' on down south
be it from a headline bold or monger's mouth.

No one was immune to news from home
(as long as warrants do not northward roam)
and thus on his rounds with mail bags bulging
Dago Joe was thus men and wives indulging.
Truth and lies, mixed, one or the other
were welcome in cabins locked in winter.

The only respite for Dago Joe
from the bite of frost and trails of snow
was a fortnight sojourn in the Bonfire Saloon
where he could drink and howl at the moon
until the Nome P.O.
had more news to travel o'er the snow.

KANGAROO JACK

Kangaroo Jack came from where boomerangs fly
forward and back across vacant skies,
over dingoes and wombats and Tasmanian beasts
and red kangaroo who on mangroves feast
along with the Abos who wander the land
from Victoria north to Queensland.

The spawn of a wastrel and chardy on plonk
who were only half-human when both were drunk,
he cut his teeth on sheep shearing and dung
which paid for the sparse clothing which hung
on his frame kept thin from the food he could eat
when he managed to steal enough on to feast.

It did not take him long to decipher the worth
of a man, nay a boy, who was from a poor birth.
To rise from the tumult of the chardy crowd
he fled to the city where he slept in the shrouds
of the dead in the morgue where he was employed
washing cadavers before they were interred.

It did not take him long to decipher the code
of the wealthy landowners and who they employed.
It was cash, always cash, whether in hand or in banks,
in land, stocks and bonds or sheep herds by the shank
so he switched occupations from soaping the dead
to washing investments in gold, silver and lead.

He began as a runner for tellers and clerks
purveying the paper that made the bank work:
notarized letters with fiscal spread sheets,
certified checks and withdrawal receipts
and occasionally cash in paper and coin
in delivery bags all to eloign.

As trust in the lad grew by steps, leaps and bounds
he graduated from pennies to bushels of pounds
all the time learning how cash in all forms
transmuted to paper and, once transformed,
was easy to carry in both pocket and purse
or hide under a mattress before it's dispersed.

Thus he did learn that cash had no place
in banking at all and thus the mad race
by most people for money – that's held in your hand –
was fabled for the wealth of the land
be it in person or county, nation or state
was in the form of certificates.

It was paper, all paper, in columns of ink,
sheet upon sheet, in both black and pink,
that measured the wealth of a person or plan
be he Frenchman, English or Australian,
woman or business, corporate or small
worth was in black ink. The sum of it all

was how you were treated. In the eyes of the world
wherever you were – man, woman or girl –
depended not on your clothing or hair on your face
it was the black numbers that determined your fate.
With the more numbers you had the more
blessings of gods,
fewer and all you got from bankers were nods.

But there was a problem, all bankers agreed,
second, of course, to slick fingers and greed,
was moving inked papers in bundles and sheets,
deposits, withdrawals, bonds and escheats,
from deep in the Outback to a bank in the town
and thereafter to Leeds avoiding the drown.

It was paper, all paper, the gods of the bank,
for money in place did not a farthing make,
so value was not the amount of cash coming in
but how it was placed by paper and pen.
This was the lesson learned by Kangaroo Jack
which he carried to Nome in an old gunny sack.

He established an office on the shelf over his bed,
printed bank cards in black ink – never red –
then plied the saloons, bunkhouses and beaches
for men with gold flakes who feared the leaches,
who would exchange their gold for a paper receipt
with the value in cash of a dead parakeet.

Alas, it was known, along the sea shore
much more elusive than finding the ore
was a way to leave Nome with the gold that you found
with the sweat of your brow in the depth of ground,
and arrive in states, East Coast or West
with your fortune intact inside your vest.

"It's harder to save than it e'er is to earn
As too many sourdoughs over time learned
so the key to success was a friend at a bank
so those who knew me knew who to thank
for transforming gold into federal dollars
worth the same in cities and hollers.

So I spend my time in the Bonfire Saloon
waiting to transfer gold nuggets soon.
The smart ones transfer a few of their grams
and I send the deposits by telegram
to other banks in the lower states;
banks in towns where their relatives wait.

Once the procedure has been proven true
and as long as there are no bugaboos
by week or by month – depends on the mine –
more money flows down the telegraph line.
For the banks in the states in June thereabouts
I'll place the actual gold on steamships headed south.

As we all know money is a most illusory thing
and gold only has value in Nome 'til the spring.
Then the doré moves its way south.
But the real fear is an adage I'll mouth.
A man can demand gold in a bank with a gun
but bankers with pens can rob everyone."

In 1903, there were no banking regulations. The FDIC, Federal Deposit Insurance Corporation, would not exist until 1933. So many banks were fraudulent that more than a few argonauts preferred to carry their gold with them when they returned home. Legitimate banks shipped their gold south in boxes like this.

Chechako Lil

Cheechako Lil needed a man like a rabbit needs carrot,
not every day but when someone could spare it.
Old in the sense she was 'not born yesterday,'
she knew perfectly well the price of the play
and confined herself to ragging
until she was back in North Carolina bragging.

That being said, she was of this world locked,
as she knew what was what and what all cost
from the price of beer, beans and onions brown
to whisky and moose meat in the round.
She knew of cost to the cent
of all she bought or had to rent.

She also knew the cost of her pirooting
both emotional and the chance of shouting
but this was Nome, as she often said,
and she was far from a woman dead
and she had her needs as do all who live
and pleasure she would both take and give.

She was a scrooge with cash and flakes
and did not a single misstep make
for she was not in Nome to wildly spend
on clothes or wine or odds and ends
for her restaurant was her cash cow
and she to make investments now.

As an ice-bound entrepreneur
she had a lock-step procedure
for dealing with the kittle cattle
who came not to eat but to prattle.
In her place, on bench or table,
you ate your meal and then skedaddled.

Her flame of the day, her nights to fill
was a claim jumper by the name of Bill.
No last name for by and by
best to let dogs asleep lie.
For his sobriquet, he chose caribou
to avoid telegraphic bugaboo.

Cheechako Lil did not give a whit
and no rumor made her snit.
She gave not a thought to fuss
for her goal was cash enough
so if a man chose to pay her way
in bar or tavern she let him pay.

On that night in the packed Saloon
Cheechako Lil came in for a brew
with Caribou Bill by her side.
They passed a table where a comment snide
was made to Bill that his wealth
had come from looting someone else's pelf.

Bill without a look acetate
placed a finger underneath the plate
and flicked it upwards sending beans
along with gravy and all in between
upward and over in a wide skyward
onto the man who'd made the comment snark.

In the span of a heartbeat the saloon did engage
in an outburst of curses, fisticuffs and rage.
Tables turned and glasses flew
as the spirit enticed more than a few
to swing upon his neighbor while they protected self
until the only one not so engaged was Charles the Twelfth.

Cheechako Lil was at the center of it all
and had no hesitation to engage in the brawl.
She grabbed a bottle from off the floor
and beaned a man as if he were a man-of-war
and she an invading sloop with cannons a' blazin'
and laid him low upon the floor upward star glazing.

The ruckus lasted long enough to attract the ire
of Whiskey Jack who with a shotgun fired
a single blast into the planks above
being sure to miss the cribs upstairs set aside for love
and Marshal Jew Bob leaning against the Bonfire wall
would later swear he had seen not a thing at all.

In the early years of the 1900s, Chicago investors funded the formation of the Council City & Solomon River Railroad to link the gold community of Solomon with Nome. The railroad was operational in 1903, but it did not last long. It was abandoned in 1907, with the engines and rail cars being left where they were when the line went bust. To this day, they are still there. Tourists can visit "The Last Train to Nowhere" outside of Nome.

Caribou Bill

Caribou Bill had meaty fists
which he used without compunction
against anyone who gave him fits
and swung in all directions
for more than self-protection.

He was a welcome companion
to those both small and meek
who entered the Saloon's canyon
for, with Bill, they could freely speak
and worry not to raise another's peak.

His soul mate was the Cast Iron Kid,
the preacher who walked saloon row
raising money for those on the skid
who had missed the Blue Ticket show
and had no place to go.

He was pleased with Cheechako Lil;
she kept him gentile
and paid his bills
at the mercantile in exchange he made the spiels
to make sure all paid for their meals.

Without Lil when he got drunk
he was as a wet dog in church
and behind his back all called him skunk
when he began to lurch
and fall off his saloon perch.

A rounder in his days
before he mouthed advice he heard,
rarely said in metaphor,
but cleansed when with his snow-bird
"Drink upstream from the herd."

Cast Iron Kid

In summer and winter, spring and fall,
on each square foot where feet fall,
there must be someone who is honest in fact
regardless the pressure on to his back
or his pocket or ego or anything else:
a man of God impervious to pelf.

Such was the case of the Cast Iron Kid
who took no advantage of those on the skid,
a regular in the Bonfire Saloon, a savior of souls,
a holy dragoon searching for those
who needed succor
and helping them stumble out of the door.

Let it never be said he was harassed or ignored,
drinker, drunkard or saloon landlord,
for everyone knew this mortal coil
was short, stinky and ignoring your moil
we would all go to some other place
one of them hot and the other one graced.

In fact, it was not odd for the Saloon
to close its servings down at noon
on every Sundays so the Cast Iron Kid
and the doc could service those on the skids
and all pitched in with flakes and coin
for no one knew for sure where they were going.

There is only truth, one guarantee,
be you a man, woman, black or Pawnee:
no one ever knows what next morning will bring.
You could be Croesus rich and ready to sing
then the wind in your sails would die in the East
leaving you broke with nothing to eat.

The best time to remember this gospel of truth
is as you wallow on forbidden fruit.
Flush with gold nuggets or pouches of flakes
you'd best be prepared for a sharp turn to take;
Whenever you feel you're loaded with bread
bad news is a' coming 'round the bend ahead.

Box Car Aggie

Box Car Aggie was a farmer by choice
because her body was perfect – not so her voice –
which made little difference in Nome's row of saloons
because man came for the women and even baboons,
if they were female, could a fortune make
off men with no brains and the morals of snakes.

Aggie she was and the field which she tilled
were row upon row of men whom she shilled
draining their pokes be they nuggets or cash
by luring them upstairs for pleasure then dash
them with a billy she'd rap on their heads
and toss their bodies out the back window dead.

It was a scheme in which she was well armed
as she had been a butcher once on the farm.
She said the thud of a billy on miners' skulls
sounded the same as an oar on the hull
of a rowboat on the cruise of an inland lake
but was a far more profitable action to take.

She didn't kill all as she always took time
to make sure she would not be caught for her crime.
She struck only those miners who worked their own claim
so there were no men to search for their partner in vain.
Then with her partner, the Limping Grouse
she'd split up the spoils between her and the house.

The two were superb in their choosing of men
who would never be missed so into their den
like flies swoop into the web of a spider
the miners succumbed to their whispers and cider.
They prowled the ice sidewalks from one end of town
to the other searching for men to lure down.

Odd it was on a hunting spree
on the ninth of December in Nineteen Ought Three,
the pair stumbled into the Bonfire Saloon
on a search, so they said, for the light of the moon,
when out of the press of the men in the hard drinking mob
stepped the man with the badge, Marshal Jew Bob.

Marshal Jew Bob well aware of the two,
of the work of the pair and the men they went through.
He'd searched for the pair along Nome's Front Street
tavern by tavern and all dark retreats
for he had a gift for those would steal:
chains running between twin hoops of steel.

Thus it was as the Bonfire Saloon
struck up the band with a guitar and bassoon,
Marshal Jew Bob with help from Socialist Kid
looped up the pair as they came in from the skid
and then Box Car Aggie and Limping Grouse
found themselves escorted uptown to the jail house.

History does not record the fate of the two
who murdered and robbed more than a few,
other than say their days they did wile
splitting the cords on the city's wood pile
until the spring sun broke the Bering Sea's ice
then with a blue ticket took the first steamer south.

Jimmy the Goat

Jimmy the Goat had a grip on the throat
    of the defendant's seated in court.
Metaphorically speaking, the man had been leaking
    rumors of the weakness of tort
that Jimmy's been selling as though the telling
    would add to the tale when told
of a man who'd been duped by a tin can of soup
    and drained of his pouch filled with gold.

"It's a sad tale," Jimmy did wail,
    "how my upstanding client got scammed.
It began with a quail with a lace-covered tail
    who promised an evening of cramming.
But as the moment of bliss arrived with the miss
    so did a man who proclaimed
he was the spouse and said, 'Who is this louse
    with whom his wife is enflamed?'

'This dynamite can I hold in my hand
    will resolve this violation of marriage
and once it is lit it will blow us to bits
    and take all of us off in a carriage
to the orchard of marble where a preacher will garble
    our names and events which transpired
in the upstairs room of the Bonfire Saloon
    and the boom in which we expired.'

"The man who was duped, had no choice to stoop
    to withdraw all the gold from his purse
to pay off the mad man with a fuse on a can
    and flee from the room with a curse
with his suspenders flying behind him trying
    to outrun the threat of a hearse.

In a fake rage pulled from the page
    of a conman's handbook of the tricks,
he used the wile of the whores to con a man in his drawers.
    Then the bogus prick
of a husband, so claimed, stated he'd been defamed
    by this act of his alleged wife
and he opened his hand to reveal a tin can
    which he said would end all their strife.

"Now the truth of the matter," Jimmy said with a swagger
    pointing to the man in a chair,
"that after the scam, you, my good man,
    laughed about how you had scared
the man in the room of the Bonfire Saloon
    with a soup can you let him assume
was a dynamite stick with a fuse of a stick
    which would kill all three with a boom.

"But the fact of the matter," Jimmy said in a lather,
    "you knew the soup can was a fraud,
for you had been drinking and downstairs slinking
    and had no gun to frighten the clod.
You threatened the fool with a fraudulent tool,
    a soup can devoid of its label,
and stormed into the room and acted buffoon
    and struck a match on the table.

And, isn't it true, post ballyhoo,
    as the fool escaped down the street,
at the scene of the crime to your partner begrimed,
    you tossed the soup can at her feet,
then said with a grin, 'Here's a package of tin
    you can use to make your own stash.
'Take it and see, if you can like me,
    use it to con a wallet of cash.'

"Then Jimmy the Goat cleared his own throat
      and with a gesture of counterfeit rage
with theatrical fury looked at the jury
      and waved the tin can in outrage
demanding they find the bloke from the mine
      had been defamed, robbed and then duped
by the promise of passion and been scammed in a fashion
      by a label-less can of soup.

HUNGRY JACK

Hungry Mike doesn't have money.
The reason is he's a dummy,
who eats his beans raw
uses burl wood for chaw
and doesn't know dung from wild honey.

Handsome Harry

Handsome Harry and Spanish Marie
were quite the pair on the Bering Sea.
He from Norway, she from Tempe
they both spoke with accents clearly
demarking their homes on the curve of the earth,
an odd marriage which had come north.

Spanish Marie had a split life;
half on the beach and the other as wife
to Handsome Harry who recorded gold claims
on and below, on rivers and streams,
and appeared as the expert for those with wealth
in the courtroom of Charles the Twelfth.

When it came to land, Nome was triple deformed,
each sector unique. As the city was formed
land on the seacoast, all miles of the sand
could not be claimed by any man
for it was owned by the feds, every square foot,
and you could only claim title to that which you took

below the high water mark. To the wetlands in back
the land was checkered in fact,
divided by roadways and sidewalks, churches and bars,
saloons, taverns and mud boulevards,
lots were determined by inch and by foot
from where lot stakes were originally put.

For the next dozens of miles beyond city streets
where the moss and the tundra had millennia creep
there was gold buried deep in the ground
left by the retreating ocean yet to be found.
claim line by spoil pile and coyote hole
miners filed papers to secure their stash of gold.

That being said, the landmarks of the claims
were often disputed and therefore the names
of who owned what was always in doubt
and he who lost out was the man without clout
and every claim which had gold flakes to deport
ended in contention before the Commissioner's court.

Hour by day by landmark and eyeline
Handsome Harry passed out the fines
to those who were digging on some other's claim
and to those others who claimed they had been defamed
by curse and invective tossed by and forth
as a hot potato followed by bellow and curse.

The syndicate case before Charles the Twelfth
involved two claimants each stealing the other's pelf.
The nitpicking had progressed both theft and exchange
until neither side knew that which remained
on either one's claim had been originally theirs
or been stole back and forth, alone or in pairs.

The dispute had begun on the banks of a stream
and progressed saloon by tavern 'til the bickering
ended up in the court of Charles Twelfth
to decided who got what portion of pelf;
odd because the sum of the dollars it seems
would buy less than a can of beans.

But both wanted a hearing, a case in a court,
for both of the clowns were intent on a tort,
since each suspected the other of vile intent
not to mention suspicion of abolishment
of every claim stake on both sides of the creek
and the absconding of flakes week after week.

As there was no pot in which tea could tempest
Charles the Twelfth put on his face best
and had Handsome Harry discuss the claim lines
with map and chart and legal designs.
With a pen the gold in dispute was beget
to a dozen saloons to pay the men's debts.

Harry dined in the Bonfire Saloon
for it offered a meal for which he always had room
though everyone else in the room turned faces green
and wondered how anyone in their right mind would lean
to a supper of fare of which no one was including
but Harry and it was a meal of blood pudding.

With his repast and wife in the same room
Harry was as happy as on flat lake was a loon
and ignoring the looks of the sourdough mob
dined on his congealment with a hearty nod
and thus did he savor it spoon after spoon
throughout the evening at the Bonfire Saloon.

Spanish Marie

"Sand, always sand, and after that sand again,
every 12 hour with the tide going out or in,
sand and then sand and then sand 'til the tide
turns and that's when I sleep. It is that I've
got a clock that starts on the 15th of June
and then pirouettes to the tune of the moon.

From the middle of June to the end of September –
it seems as long as I can remember –
I dug and then sifted the sands of the beach
looking for nuggets and gold flakes to keep.
You can't lay a claim on the beach sands
for no one owns the square feet where they stand.

For those of you who are not in know,
the stretch of the beach from high tide below
are federal lands and cannot be staked as a claim
so anyone with a pan who will suffer the pain
of digging and sluicing and cursing half-day
can sleep soundly if their square footage pays.

During the summer I stream with the rest
out onto the sands and try my best
to sift what I can from the golden beach sands then,
with the coming of winter, my duties expand
to that of the wife with social demands
in support of my husband who surveys the land.

From freeze-up to thaw, I pour tea and serve crumpets
to the wives whose husbands respond to the trumpet
of duty and honor on paper, on shelves or walking the street
with a badge and a pistol the tranquil to keep.
My husband's the man who records all the claims
from the Norton Sound shore to the fourth beach's remains.

He must be precise for the simplest of reasons:
the interior mines can only be worked in one season
and the gold that will tumble in *tsunami* amounts
must pay for all labor, ore cars and assay counts
so the mistake of a foot on the face of the earth
will down below be another's dearth.

I live in two worlds, depending the season,
in winter well-dressed I have every reason
to support my husband in his professional life
and so I am therefore a supportive wife
but only until the first week of June
when the ice sheet is broken by the phase of the moon.

Then I become a hard-core prospecting bitch
who fights for each foot I have an itch
to sift through the sands with determined moil
for what Mother Nature has left in the soil
for a dozen hours of sweat and then of retreat
for another 12 hours to sleep, curse and eat.

Unlike the others who dig gold and run
south to the states when the fall sun
sinks lower and lower and winter arrives
I stay here in Nome among the wives
of the men who work the year round
on the frozen shores of Norton Sound.

In a few years I will go back –
'Thank you very much, Kangaroo Jack'
– a woman who earned wealth by the sweat of her brow
and converted as much as she would allow
into banking paper good in the south
where my wealth backs the tales from my mouth.

At this precise moment, because of the moon,
I am stuck here in the Bonfire Saloon,
smiling at matrons and watching the clock
and pretending my interest in all the talk
but dreaming of days yet to come
when I will be long gone from this humdrum."

The nearest forest to Nome is 200 miles away. This meant every board needed for construction came north by barge from Seattle – but only from June to September. Argonauts without a lot of money had to make do with what they could scavenge, like this man, who built his hovel with abandoned lumber, canvas, chunks of sheet metal, and any tree limbs which had been swept in by storms. Note the chimney sticking out of the top of the structure. Nine months out of the year, he had to burn coal to stay warm – and that coal had to be shipped into Nome from Seattle.

DIAMOND DICK

Diamond Dick wears fine clothes.
How he pays for them nobody knows.
He'll steal from a store
anything not nailed to the floor
including a red hot stove.

WHISKEY JACK

Whiskey Jack didn't want to go back
but then again he couldn't
for wherever he'd been he left with the sin
    of doing things he shouldn't.
On Frisco Bay he'd made the dismay
    of the local constabulary
with rattling cuffs he knew that he must
    find another sanctuary.

Mad as a cat in a baptismal bath
    he gave the bluecoats the slip
and headed to Nome as his newfound home
    when he stowed on a northbound ship.
A bar dog by day he knew all the right ways
    whiskey could be served in mugs
in the buckets of blood where he had withstood
    fisticuffs, coppers and drugs.

Never a receiver of barrel fever
    and he had never been in the sun
he filled in for a sot who had gone to pot
    and threatened a drunk with a gun
in the Bonfire Saloon and by the next noon
    he had quelled three disputes and a thug
who was selling bottles of ale to an Eskimo male
    claiming it was a medicinal drug.

The thug had a job, said Marshal Jew Bob,
    to please some distant in-law
by selling moonshine, a glass for a dime,
    which was violation of law.
Thus did Whiskey Jack with a smile and blackjack
    escort the thug from the room
then knocked the man silly with the caress of his billy
    and earned him a job in the saloon.

Whiskey Jack was no fool, he knew all the rules,
    but he knew how to milk a cow
so he set about to profit throughout
    his shifts with his criminal knowhow.
He took a cut from the rooms upstairs in the saloon,
    he ordered the whiskey in bulk
and took a kickback from Peg Legged Jack
    and doubled the cost of moose hulk.

With fastidious care he made sure his hair
    was firmly attached to its base.
With grease it held tight and all through the night
    he would pat it to keep it in place.
Everyone paid in gold so as each patron was sold
    whiskey with a pinch of gold flake,
and some of the gold sand stuck to his hand
then a pat of his hair he did make.

At the end of his shift, loaded with gifts
    courtesy of his greased strands
he'd return to his room and with a broom
    sweep the flakes into a pan.
And just like a miner he spent a whole hour
    carefully extracting the flakes
of the gold he'd taken care to stick to the grease on his hair
    and added it to his hourly take.

Rabbit Nose Bob

Rabbit Nose Bob, always on the job,
was the salt of the earth
rather, it's said, what it was he spread
increased the worth of the dirt.
With a shotgun in hand he'd fire gold sand
into a virginal lot
so the speckles of gold would get the lot sold
and he would make quite a lot.

From his poke of gold flakes, frauds he would make
and leave town before the next spring,
when the rube with the land would find only gold sand
and not one other valuable thing.
He had started in Dawson when the fines
had been awesome – the real ones, not those he had
faked – then he headed west avoiding arrest
by boomtown, dupe and false flakes.

It could never be said he got out of bed
without a scheme on his mind
be it counterfeit bills, fictional stills
or a treasure map to a lost mine.
He spent all his days in a villainous haze
searching for rubes to misuse,
be he sickened or hale he could swallow square nails
and spit them all out in corkscrews.

A boomer, a boozer, a false witness excuser,
he pulled his first scam in St. Pete.
as a young lad he proved so exquisitely bad
a rival gang took out his front teeth.
Boarding a train he headed for Maine
but ended up in Detroit
where even they were shocked and dismayed
how flagrant he was to exploit

the rich and the poor, then a state senator,
which, as all knew was a switch,
for he was in office only to profit
and it was a hoot he'd been snitched.
But the coppers weren't laughing as they had been passing
corruption dollars for ages.
It went from bad to worse when Bob took to verse
exposing elected outrages.

Again on the run, this time with a gun,
he headed north where the sun
dies for the night and is reborn when its light
runs through the streets of Dawson.
If ever a place composed of disgrace
for law and the rule of decorum
it was here on the shore of the Yukon River
and in the close by environs.

Thanking the gods, Rabbit Nose Bob,
believed he found felonial heaven
for the marshal was blind and the pickings were fine
and every dice roll was eleven.
All rivers have bends and all halcyon ends
and Dawson was no anomaly
when boom went to bust Rabbit Nose cussed
on the last steamship down to the sea.

On St. Mary's shore he had to explore
which direction was best for his health,
south were the states and telegram dates
from courts drooling to try him for stealth.
The only course that remained was the Bering Sea main
to Nome dodging bergs of ice
where he was dumped overboard by a crew who'd
been gored by his marked cards and treasonous dice.

He spent his first summer being a bummer
selling claim lots salted with flakes
and sold shares in ghost stills and the sales went well
until it was discovered a fake.
Then he collected gold ore from a family of four
whose father had been downed by the plague
and fled with the cash in a mad Nome-ward dash
when it was discovered the fund had goose-egg.

The greatest blessing when it came to be guessing
where a conman could be hiding
was the size of the town which stretched far beyond
the six blocks of the saloon-front sidings.
So Rabbit Creek Bob would avoid the mad mobs
searching for the absconded cash
until winter blew in and winter's grim grin
forced Bob to bury his cache.

But that afternoon in the Bonfire Saloon
eschewing the snow-chocked street,
Marshal Jew Bob with a writ from the mob
by those who swore it was cheat
for Rabbit Nose Bob to collect and then rob
a family of four never born.
"You're over the line, I suggest you resign,
you got the wrong pig by the tail.

There's nowhere to dash so hand over cash
or you'll spend the next eight months in jail …
". . . where the warmest of days until the next May
is 30 below even in togs
which it is sad to say, it blows every day
through all the chinks in jail logs.
Your fast talking deceit has snagged you complete
and here you can't pack bags and scoot.
So be a good fellow and cough up the yellow
or you'll be wearing an Oregon boot."

Rabbit Nose Bob stopped his hobnob
in the warmth of the Bonfire Saloon
and scrambled outside, perhaps to hide
in a cabin on the far side of the moon.
But where the galoot beat feet to scoot
mattered not the forces of good
for if he ever came back there was cot with a sack
with his name etched deep in the wood.

When Marshal Jew Bob was asked of Rabbit Nose Bob
the Marshal's words were quite plain,
Rabbit Nose Bob was a con who hobnobbed
with folks who gave him no pain
then he drained them of gold on stories he told
pretending to be a god send.
"He's the lowest of scum and we should be glad he's run
for only buzzards feed on their friends."

THE DOUGHNUT QUEEN

When she plays hide-and-seek
the Doughnut Queen's at her peak.
But when she wants water
she must call her daughter
to not scare water from the creek.

SAWDUST KING

"He is the Sawdust King for good reason.
His railroad script is as worthless
as steel shavings trying to be passed as gold.

None of us take script. The Bonfire Saloon and
Roulette Joe and Cast Iron Kid only take
script Kangaroo Jack accepts because
Windy Smith says some bank in some god
forsaken city in some damned state will pay gold
for the script it cannot see and does not have.

This is the story of the railroad. It is new here this year.
In Solomon. Just down the beach. It is a pipe dream.
But it is typical of the Alaska dream. Take
something used, us, the men who are normal
anywhere else, used and abused, and try your luck
in Alaska, as far as you can go, from wherever
you are from, and still speak English.

The railroad is used property out of New York.
Where I came from.
New York did not value me.
New York did not value the rail cars.
Both of us are here, at the end of a road, together.

Roads are what you make of them. There was no place
for me in New York.
Only money made the difference.
A three-eyed mule would be welcome in New York
if it had a million dollar collar.

I don't need a million dollar collar
to be welcome here.
I just have be not normal
here because none of us here
fit in anywhere else.

We are in it together,
here, the railroad and me,here,
in the frontier where you do not have to
be normal. Because if you were,
you would not be here."

SLAUGHTERHOUSE MIKE

It was always a wonder in the Bonfire Saloon
how Slaughterhouse Mike
could pay for his whiskey and steak.
He was not a rich man, judging by his clothes,
and even in a town where everyone knew
what was in every telegram,
no one knew where his cash came from.

Who was giving Slaughterhouse Mike
gold and script and cash was unknown.
What was known was his pension for
being a nasty drunk. Salt of the earth, mild-mannered
and amiable in church and on the street, but it
only took a single drink to make him mean
enough to eat off the same plate as a snake.

It only took one rude remark to set him on a spree
with flying fists and more often than not he would say,
"When I'm done with you, there won't be enough to snore."
He suffered no katzenjammers For every tomorrow
he was the same as last night – before the first whiskey.

When he died of some unknown affliction –
– alcohol was the suspect,
It was said by one man, yet applauded by all,
that one should only say good of those who have died.
"The sonofabitch is dead," the man said, "Good."

Two Step Louie

Two Step Louie had no place to go
his wife had proved a bust
then he'd become hooked on snow
and the gold he come to trust
as it never looked at him in disgust.

He'd learned how to live on beans
salmon, moose and grouse
and panned enough to fuel his dreams
and pay for a ramshackle house
shared with many a mouse.

He had a thirst for dancing
'Turkey in the Straw'
and went saloon prancing
and with muddied boots trod
where're he gave the band a wad.

There was no place for Louie
in the lower states
he declared himself an refugee
or, perchance, an emigrate,
where there was no standard state.

He loved the life he chose,
a decision he deemed wise,
and cared not for his clothes
and cared less for his demise,
and let the mice eat his eyes.

Tommy the Rat

Tommy the Rat had a favorite stoop
next to the entry of the trollop's coop
where he worked paper magic with Aces and Eights:
Ace for the house and Eight for the straights
who dreamed to increase their take in gold flakes
from a cardsharp with the ethics of a snake.

A dream is something you sweat to achieve;
fantasies are the domain of make-believe,
succor for those days when you've lost all your hope
and wallow in the drudgery of fried beans and soap,
when every dawn ends with a setting sun
and birthdays are markers for failures undone.

Tommy the Rat offered the lure of the quick wealth
without the sweat of the brow or revolver with stealth;
the delusion of luck with a handful of cards
a'seat in a warm room with no hoist of petard,
to free you from the confusions of strife,
to wallow in wealth the rest of your life.

Be it Faro or Monte, Poker or Craps,
Blackjack or Hazard, he'd take all your cash,
nuggets and script, which he'd sweep off the felt
as fast as a pot falling off of a shelf
in a log cabin in a temblor shake
leaving nothing but shards the size of snowflakes.

But it must be said that Tommy the Rat
was the personification of his own caveat.
He spent every dime and nugget of gold
on whiskey and women and when told
he should save for the day the Bonfire closed
he said 'Balderdash' to what was proposed.

Tommy the Rat, like the bulk of the crowd,
squandered to make the devil proud.
All firmly believed their ship had come in
(so what was the harm indulging in sin?)
for they would stay wealthy day after day
and no day of reckoning would 'er come their way.

George Franklin Wade had an astonishing record of both criminal activity and escapes. He was convicted of selling opium in 1891 but escaped in March of 1892. He was recaptured and, after his release, two years later, was found guilty of possessing "two trunks containing about one hundred pounds" of opium. He was sentenced to McNeil Island – the maximum-security federal prison on the West Coast – where he escaped in July of 1894. In 1904 he was convicted in Nome for stealing gold from sluices and sent to McNeil Island. Then, on the morning of July 4, 1905, he engineered an escape with seven other prisoners, the largest escape in the history of McNeil Island. Surprisingly, the men dug tunnels from cell to cell with spoons and then breached the prison's outer wall. The seven who escaped with Wade were recaptured, some on the mainland. Wade was not.

The School Marm

"I spend my time in public school
and teach the young the three Rs
which all will need as dollars rule
in mines in stores and hearths.
Those who venture to my class
are smart enough to know
anyone can scavenge brass by digging through the snow.

My students smell like fish and beans
and soot from Yukon stoves,
but that does not stand between their minds
and mining goaf.
Native, white, black and brown,
I teach the children of the town.

To meet the mining schedule
I start my school at noon
and on my bike I peddle to the Bonfire Saloon
here some of my waifs linger in company of hard men
who give me the upright finger as though
I was an alderman.

There is not space in student brains
for chaff and fairy tales
for they must for the future train in
law firms or on railroad rails.
I will never know if I've done my service well;
But years from now my success will surely tell."

Waterfront Brown

Waterfront Brown had a lust for wealth
in the form of flakes or script
from the thefts he embezzled with stealth
in the form of freight from ships.

As lighterage lord he burgled the barges
bringing the cargo that came ashore
and stored all the goods for winter discharge
which he peddled door to door.

He was the patron saint of stevedores
who offloaded the steamers and ships
and squirreled away freight from all the wharves
and paid for the tonnage in script.

His recollections were faulty
when it comes to the receipts of his trade
be it apples or pork bulk salty,
apples, pans or butcher knife blades.

If you wanted it he got it,
but only sells his ill-gotten gains
when the last of the steamships have split
leaving Nome frozen in again.

He prowls the saloons and taverns
for miners exhausted of beans
who for pork thighs they yearn
along with butter and nicotine.

The Bonfire needs his service
because his product is stored by the ton.
He believes it's entrepreneurial cowardice
to cut prices 'til the winter's done.

His cognizance is his order form,
his memory is sharp as a tack
until Marshal Jew Bob wants him to inform
on his navy of mountebanks.

Tripod Pete

Tripod Pete was as black as raven feathers
and few there were who could not call him brother
for he was the man who everyone called
when it came time for a convenience stalled,
be it for pipes or windows, stoves or stools,
he was the master of all which required tools.

He came from two lines of soldiers in blue
who fought Johnny Reb and then the Sioux.
Brothers in arms they traded sisters;
Pete's uncle became a surgeon's assister
while Pete's father chose to drive railway spikes
from Missouri west to the Peak of Pike's.

As the rail lines stretched west so did the crew
of Pete and his kith and kin too
first Missouri then Denver to Reno and beyond
swinging hammers and singing songs.
But Pete had a hankering to see the rest
of the world so he packed a bag and headed west.

His homestead was a bust so he tried nugget mining
in the wilds of Nevada where he found slim findings.
He spent so many years on his sagebrush claim
he knew all of the lizards by their first name.
Then he got smart and switched to fixing machines
with wrench, screw driver and rags with benzine.

More money is made by merchants than miners
was the lesson he learned while fixing diners,
from foundation to shingles and privies to wells,
steam engine on the *fritz* and stalled carousels.
He was in San Francisco as a fixer with tools
when the Nome strike dominated the news.

A syndicate formed from where he was employed
and his passage was certain as he was family devoid
so he and his tools on the ship *Rosalie* steamed
north on the Pacific and thence Bering Sea.
But in Unalaska the steamer's boiler went cold
and Pete spent three days before it could again burn coal.

In those three days he acquired such fame
that everyone knew of his tools and his name
so when they reached Nome there was no doubt
he would never lack for employment throughout
Nome or with mines on the tundra remote,
or the saloons, buildings or even steamboats.

His sobriquet came from a task on the fly
when a photographer needed bracing to try
a long-timed snapshot when the lighting was poor
so Pete fashioned a tripod from flotsam on shore,
waterlogged trusses and branches in place,
secured in a tripod with a camera brace.

The photograph appeared in newspaper pages
from Seattle to Denver and then in stages
down both the coasts, West and East,
giving fame to the name of Tripod Pete.
He drank not a drop of the swill from stills
but was welcomed in all saloons for his skills.

Those skills were used around the clock
in the mines where he repaired ore locks,
steam engine valves and tumbler grating,
plumbing pipes and time clock stamping.
If it ran or flowed, spewed or grew
he proved himself the doodad *guru*.

That December in Nineteen Ought Three
he was called to fix a jammed latrine.
It's latch cord was a bust leaving the pedal
frozen in place and then the ice gripped the metal
so human hands had to reach beneath the plate
to thaw out the hinges and corrections make.

Tripod Pete was called to the task,
overtime, double time plus a thanks
in cash he could deposit in a bank
for they wanted him to be more than thanked
for machines are never a saloon's friend
and a man like Pete would be needed again.

Pete refused to take a Saloon brew,
an elixir he had for decades eschewed,
asked instead for tea and solace
as he rubbed the payment in his pocket,
he said in jest to Happy Jack
as he slapped the Native on his back,

"Gold in streambeds is your gig;
for gold in privies it's how I dig."

For most argonauts, the gold in Nome was in the beach sand. No one could stake a claim on the beach because it was federal property. However, it was legal to search for gold on the beach, so the only land you could 'mine' was within reach of your shovel. And only during the 12 hours of the day when the tide was out.

ROULETTE JOE

Roulette Joe was the man with the pen
in the Nome General Store –when open.
Business was brisk when the tide water was in
but when it went out he had no for use poison pen
and you'd find him in the Bonfire Saloon
drinking his profits and singing a tune.

This was the season for mittens and boots
rarely for parkas because every galoot
who missed the last steamer to cities below
had bought a parka before the first snow.
In winter the cost of a parka was through
the roof like whiskey 90 proof.

Roulette Joe was both Jap and Chink
and sold everything from nuts to sinks.
As thin as a snake erect on stilts
he was as adroit as the rest of his ilk
and set his prices by whomever came in
one for the suckers and lowered for kin.

With the Cast Iron Kid he was linked at the hip
supplying the mission until the first ship
would bring eleemosynary relief to the north
and Roulette Joe never calculated the worth
because what he lost to the those on the street
was swallowed by increases on his spread sheet.

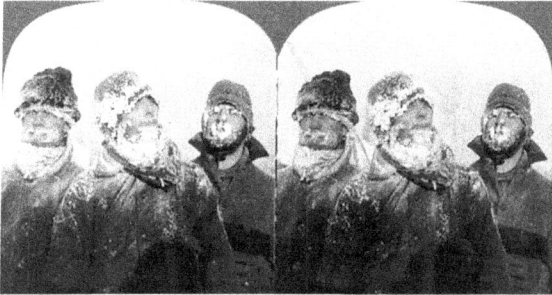

SHORT AND DIRTY

Short and Dirty always lived down to her name,
on both alley and street she had her fame
as rude and outspoken on her very best days,
ill-tempered, dyspeptic, sotted and braying
she could be found where opportunity loomed
which, in December, was the Bonfire Saloon.

She had the sense of buzzard on carrion campaign
giving every indication of being insane.
She wore vestments so whorish it left no one doubt
as to her profession when she was out and about.
Her expressions were Southern from down by the sea
and she started her day with a pint of whiskey.

She fit like a glove with the argonaut crowd
squeezing profit from sweat and not being proud
about saving a dime or, in her case, a buck,
whenever and wherever she gave men a luck.
She been drinking her way all through her thirties
in a profession which left her life short and dirty.

She had no box herder to share in her booty
and there was no Line in Nome for the snooty
to whisper 'those women' are kept on 'that side'
while they sat in a pew with an attitude snide.
With mercury she was well acquainted
and rarely was her face painted.

It was often said and most probably true
that far from her room she was laid on residue
of the privies beneath the floor of the saloon's din
which remained as glaciers of urine
well into June when the return of the Norton Sound tide
took the glaciers of urine on a westward ride.

She was not welcome in the Bonfire Saloon
for the box herder had his own girls to groom.
Short and Dirty was not welcome inside
for she sullied the floorshow of the nide.
Her presence raised the bar keepers' ire
and they would not piss on her put out a fire.

Not to be deterred that December eve
Short and Dirty shed not a tear of grieve,
she simply sequestered Slaughterhouse Mike
on his way in with a poke and a pike.
None of the barkeeps cared even a whit
for Slaughterhouse Mike never gave tips.

And off the pair went, stumbling in snow
for some secure corner out of the blow
where he would trade the wealth of his poke
for a moment of pleasure and then, when broke,
Short and Dirty would leave him as though
he was a road apple froze solid in snow.

Long Shorty

Long Shorty was cunning as a red pig running,
    he was always fishing and not cutting
bait 'cause in the mine you had to dig through the fines
    an' you had to root hog or die, Jake.
He gave the devil his due and then drank devil's brew
    and if you disturbed him while he was asleep,
lickety split he'd grab you by the neck
    and kick you into next week.

Long Shorty was a mucker, a tunnel bore sucker,
    who swung a pick eight hours a day
in the Solomon Mines for not enough dimes
    to support his Bonfire habit with pay.
A colorful lout he used expressions throughout
    each binge at the Bonfire Saloon
from the mines in Montana, the bars in Savannah,
    and in Frisco fights with the Muldoons.

"Hell bent for election" he said of the selection
of men seeking to be mayor,
"dreadful knowin' critters," "stiff-necked old buggers"
    who "didn't know enough carry guts to a bear."
"Tough as a biled owl" he was in the Bonfire to howl
    at his age it was all he could do and from the
    way he drank liquor he was on the road to hell
    quicker than those who husbanded their brew.

Men in the mines were a breed resigned
　　to die in an underground grave,
at the drop of hat they could be blown flat
　　and a tunnel could become a dark cave.
After years of drudgery he had beat the skullduggery
　　of the pinks, the bulls and the pigs,
who smoked fine cigars they kept in glass jars
　　while men lost their life in the digs.

The mine has just opened and Long Shorty was hopin'
　　this would be his last rodeo,
an expression he learned from a cowboy named Bern
　　when they shared a jail cell in Reno
when he punched an old bull and
knocked out the numbskull.
　　Bern had a similar target;
as late one night with a lariat tight
　　he had punched a bull all the way to a market.

Scotch Albert

Scotch Albert was most aptly named
and he was never broke.
His was a straight forward game
which started when he woke.
then spent 'til folks thought him broke.

Scotch Albert was a nigger
who came with family money.
He drank the best in jiggers
and none of his cash was phony
which produced no acrimony.

Scotch Albert's hands were scorched
from undertaker's lye.
In daylight hours he searched for those
who would soon lie
in a coffin they had to buy.

A silent wolf against the moon
he'd eyeball all the boozers
dead drunk in Nome saloons
keeping track of losers
and opium misusers.

From September until June
clients lay in repose
in his warehouse storage room
while Albert sold their clothes
until they were unfroze.

He then earned his livelihood
to melt the denizens
and stack them in cords like wood
in a vat, a liquid prison,
until one and all were wizened.

Back to chest and chest to back
he'd stand them in a hole
and squeeze them in, this maniac,
and with a pastoral cajole
he'd then fill up the hole.

To those who found his work crazy
or maybe even ghoulish
he said he was far from lazy.
"No one ever found me foolish
and when it comes to the interred,
a complaint I've never heard."

ROTTEN EGG MIKE

Rotten Egg Mike, with a cleaver in hand,
worked the lunch counter in Maryland,
in the meanest block of all downtown
where the sun in the sky never went down
or ever came up. It was so dark
the only light came from matchstick sparks.

Michael Flanagan was out of his class,
ambitious in thought but lacking in brass,
and anything else that could be turned into cash
because he had been gutted in the 95 Crash
and like all of others who stumbled those streets
he was lucky to work to buy food to eat.

He had started his life in a maritime brood
with your income secure and so was your food.
You could start as a youngster aboard any ship
and work your way upward to full mate or slip
onboard the hull of a boat seeking lobster or cod,
and fear only the mercurial wrath of sea gods.

Odd it was he suffered the landlubber disease of motion
sickness and the waves brought out the sneeze
which turned to distress in both his head and his bowels
and both knees went weak on calm days or in howls
so he chose as a profession to labor on shore
as a dock hugging, hard drinking stevedore.

It was not easy, this work on the dock
where all cargo comes in by the cask or the box
which were lifted on onboard by nettings of rope
and offloaded the same way with always the hope
that the off coming numbers matched on the sheet
the volume of cargo so no filcher could cheat.

All had been well until 93
when two large employers went under a tree
and the *tsunami* of panic swept east to New York
where the stock market went under like a cork
secured to the rocks in the bowels of sea
with the tide coming in by double digit degrees.

In the blink of an eye the nation went black
– red as the bankers say when dollars you lack —
leaving the masses of working men on the street
with no work and no money and nothing to eat.
So Michael Flanagan was blessed, it is true,
had a job to buy food but not a drop of brew.

In a job going nowhere at the dead end of a line
of double track disaster he was stalled with a dime;
no chance to move forward and he could not go back
so there he stood with a cleaver 12 hour a day to hack
meat from the carcass of pork, beef and lamb
with no chance to make money except with a scam.

It was more than a matter of draining the till,
it was what you did next avoiding the spill
of bad luck and coppers and penitentiary time
which years later would leave him without a dime
afloat on the street with no chance of a job
to rot in an alley like a year old corn cob.

But God has a way, or perhaps it is Satan,
who opens odd doors for the purpose of taking
a chance that occurs but once in each life
to let you escape your condition of strife.
A syndicate going west needed a cook
so Michael saw a chance and became a crook.

The night before the farmers went west,
Flanagan put the fill of the till into his vest.
Then the next morning precisely at eight
he hopped aboard as syndicate freight
heading west ever west to Oregon's coast
where he would be in charge of slaughtering goats.

There is an old saw which proves itself true
that bad luck never leaves no matter where you
call your home or whatever your profession
for it follows you forever in procession.
What goes out will surely again come around
until you find peace in the graveyard ground.

The long arm of the law, though slow in extension,
gradually reached the goat herders' convention
and snagged Flanagan with the iron grip of the court
adding to that the paperwork of a tort.
Sitting in jail he was given a choice
run to Alaska or spend six years in the joint.

An Alaskan quip which has no retort:
"Never fail to not ask why someone came north.
Accept no letters from the town of your birth
and when your true name comes up chuckle with mirth
and say 'That's not me, I swear that it's true,
my real name is John Smith. I'm from Kalamazoo."

Flanagan did not have that far to run
for the ships going north left from Portland
so he stowed aboard a steamer in port
and only came out when too far to the north
for the ship to turn back. Since he could cook
he was chained the stove and slept in a nook.

Once in Nome he went over the rail
floating ashore gripping the tail
of a lightering barge loaded with bags,
suitcases and casks and gaming hall swag.
But it didn't take long for him to learn to his ire
he had jumped out of the pan and into the fire.

Nome was a place where there wasn't much work
except if you carried a pistol and dirk
and there was no place for you to run.
You were stuck in the northland as long as the sun
was up and if you were broke on the first day of fall
you were sent south chained to a ball.

The winters in Nome were long, cold and dark
and without food they are far from a lark.
Rotten Egg Mike without job or workshop
feared paperwork from a Baltimore cop
for those without cash would be in a drouth
and get Blue Ticket fare on a steamship headed south.

After a week of starvation at the tail end of June
he got a job as a cook in the Bonfire Saloon
saving his bacon while cooking the same
and thus acquired his sobriquet name
making less in the Norton Sound city of Nome
then he had been making as a cook back home.

He was trapped by his past and locked in as cook
with no hope of a new job by hook or by crook.
He could not run to the south or dip into the till
for Nome was too small to stay hidden until
a steamer left port or anywhere to the south
so he kept cooking and put a lock on his mouth.

There is an old saying, true to this day,
that both good and evil have their own way.
Both travel in cycles and return where they began
rewarding the good and giving evil the brand.
You reap what you sow be it harvest or pain,
for the cycle you start will return again and again.

Claw Hammer Bill

Claw Hammer Bill came from New York,
from the darkest blocks where you lived with a dirk,
where life was short, dirty and brutish
be you a New Yorker, Frenchman or British.
Crime wasn't a thing one could avoid
but a neighborhood passion broadly employed.

New York was seething from the docks to downtown
with people of red, white, swarthy and brown,
Gringos and Beaners, Frogs, Mickies and WOPSs
Christ Killers and Chinks, jiggers and Wogs.
Each had their own turf, their own street and sidewalk
etched clearly with blood as though lines of chalk.

The Italian Paul Kelly, an odd ethnic pairing,
ran the Gang of Five Points only sparing
any man, woman or child of Irish descent
as long, be it said, they did not have a cent
for the lifeblood of the gangs was cash ever cash
and faces God made for gang members to smash.

Claw Hammer Bill was a youth in the day
when the Gang of Five Points was swept away
by a progression of villains, alone and in pairs,
who swallowed the Five Points Gang's wares,
ruled by Monk Eastman, a bouncer and thug
well known for his bloated face like a pug.

Claw Hammer Bill was adept with the tool
which gave him his name and, as a rule,
he offered no quarter to those who he slew
and picked their pockets clean as the blood flew.
Ruthless he was but with a single brain cell
which was often asleep or suspended in jell.

At the height of his terror in December Ought One
secure that his terror would not be undone
he was lured to a crime by the Pinkertons
who wanted his reign of terror be done
but he slipped loose of their cuffs and hotfooted the town
in a box car with chickens for Illinois bound.

Murders are founded in four causes dear
money or love, anger or fear.
One can be a mistake which the law might forgive
but when in the dozens one is fugitive
so Chicago did not want the heat of the law
to descend on its streets, springtime or fall.

So Claw Hammer Bill, by that name well known.
was put with a syndicate on its way to Nome
where Bill would work as the heavy and thug
to protect the mine's acreage, water and sludge
be it thick with gold flakes or lacking a color
from the 15th of July until icebergs thundered.

All knew his name but none knew his rage
for in Nome for all winter they were all in a cage
locked tight by the ice across Norton Sound.
There was only one man with a badge in the town
And those who caused trouble with claw manner or knife
vanished from Nome as day chases night.

So Claw Hammer Bill transformed to bar fly and charmer
because he knew it was more certainly warmer
in the blast of the stove in the Bonfire Saloon
then it was in a snowbank staring up at the moon.
Nome had a code you ought never break:
Follow the rules or a cadaver you make.

Marshal Jew Bob

Blind as a bat was Marshal Jew Bob
when it came to one legal part of his job;
twice a month it occurred, on the 1st and 15th
when arrest warrants from the south were received
naming people he knew whose morals were clean
– in Nome – but whose actions below were obscene.

Wearing a badge in the North is quite odd
because of the landscape, weather and frauds.
The Bering Sea's frozen from September to June,
leaving felons free to whistle a tune
until the back country streams their ice load ungirds
and miners stampede east like a buffalo herd.

Once out of Nome there is a great throng
of gold seekers with sluices, pans and long toms.
The men scrambling inland leave you no doubt;
you break the rules here you'll never come out.
Beyond Nome to the Canadian Border
there's wasn't much law but plenty of order.

If you proved yourself unwilling to change
the behavior on warrants on which you were named,
summer, winter, springtime or fall,
you were told to beat feet or the hatchet would fall
and you would be shipped to the prison outside
where escaping was rare and most inside died.

In Nome, if you could not keep your nose clean
or committed acts which were considered obscene
you were sentenced to serve the town for a while
reducing logs to splinters on the city's wood pile.
To keep you from running your boots were sequestered
and in summer, clouds of mosquitoes did fester.

As ice began forming across Norton Sound
Marshal Jew Bob began making the rounds.
First came the collection of cash from the folk
who wanted the derelicts gone from the north.
The cash was then used as the ice sheet thickened
for one-way passage south so-called "Blue Tickers."

131

The curse of the law is knowing the truth
but not having the right to go beyond sleuth
because when a man of law goes bad
there's not much to be done, so sad,
and there are certain outrages you have to absorb
and live with the bile and or drop overboard.

At one time a deputy man of the law
was Wilson Mizner who chose to outlaw.
He once hid a bandit and, with a smile,
refused to admit it and, all the while,
stashed forty thousand of Canadian cash
and refused to give up his ill-gotten cache.

Marshal Jew Bob got news from the east
that two hooligans had pulled a deceit.
Scurvy Bill along with Two-Tooth Mike
had purloined the gold then taken a hike,
hotfooted west as far as they could go
and holed up in Mizner's cabin in Nome.

A posse was formed and but it came with a flaw:
to be legal it needed a man of the law
to guide all their action and record the whole deal
so no other *bandito* would try the same steal.
So Mizner went along with the charade
and joined the posse at the head of the parade.

Mizner, a step ahead of the crew,
salted a route for the men to pursue.
A trail of blood lead to an abandoned abode
where Mizner, alone, to the front door strode,
armed with a cigar and nothing more
he boldly kicked open the log cabin door.

Hailed for boldness for his cabin advance
no one in the posse considered the chance
that Mizner had played them for Scurvy Bill
and Two Tooth Mike who went over the hill
and neither was ever heard from again
or, for that matter, the payroll Canadian.

Marshal Jew Bob was nobody's fool,
to follow the money was his forensic rule.
Scurvy Bill and the man with two teeth
did not leave Nome with the money or wreath
therefore the gold was where they'd last slept
and the boldness of Mizner was a clue to theft.

Money, like fire, is an excellent slave
but if a master takes you to the grave.
The same can be said of the bedrock of law
if it doesn't work for you it's a duplicitous maw
which gnashes its teeth in the direction of wealth
and corrupts the ethos of the everyone's health.

Mizner left Nome supposedly broke.
Oddly, it seems, Lady Luck then awoke
and Mizner bought land in southern climes
leaving to wonder if justice was blind
but no one had proof to Mizner impugn
so all was just talk in the Bonfire Saloon.

Ham Grease Jimmy

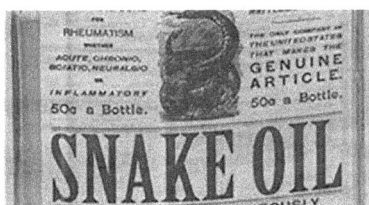

Ham Grease Jimmy had a cure
for every ailment, rash and sore.
Be it Kilmer's Swamp Root or Indian Root Pills
he had an elixir for every known ill
from gout to warts and wounds to aches
he had a cures by the vile you could take.

He had "infant soothers" for the child
and for those headaches mild
and for those consistent pains
there was a dash of cocaine
and for the ladies thick with child
there was mercury – taken mild.

"I've got a cure for every ache,
sniffle, puke or shiver-shake,
VD, cancer, cholera, pregnancy
or inflamed pleura, abscess
or rot from bullet wounds
I've got what will you keep you from the tomb.

Bonnore's Electro Magnetic Bathing Fluid
will cure all disease save in-law Druids,
Solar Tincture and Radam's Microbe Killer
will do more than be stomach fillers
but clean you out from top to bottom
every day from spring to autumn.

Pleurisy, tuberculosis,
epilepsy and psychosis,
Scarlet fever and slash infections
hip disease and skin eruptions,
if whiskey proves not the cure,
I'll sell you something better sure.

I have a special table here
in the Bonfire Saloon's atmosphere,
where my clients will attest
my bottled cures are the best
I've got a cure for every ache
to keep you above snakes."

The Pure Food and Drug Act did not pass until 1907. In 1903, "the manufacture, sale, or transportation of adulterated or misbranded or poisonous or deleterious foods, drugs or medicines, and liquors" was legal. Historically speaking, the term "snake oil" comes from the actual oil of the Chinese water snake. Chinese workers on the Southern Pacific Railway used the substance to treat arthritis and bursitis. It worked. The patent medicine industry appropriated the term to sell products that did not work.

HAPPY JACK

Happy Jack was no fool
and he had never been to school.
Barabara born and on salmon raised
he understood history had turned a page
and when the flood of men with pans and greed
swept into Nome he changed his breed.

No one cared if his skin was brown
for it was not the man's shade in town
that made the difference. It was the color
and weight of his flakes that gave him galore
and be he chink or Mex, black, white or tanned
it was the gold weight that mattered not the man.

Happy Jack could see the writing on the wall
because he learned to read and write. The fall
the stampeders came ashore in hordes
and those who said reading bored
let themselves in banks and games of gin
be skinned by men who took their gold and grinned.

Reading was more than a skill;
it was the only way to beat the bill
of ongoing banking regulations
which nipped at profit of every station,
rich man, poor man, beggar man, thief
and all the rest of those in-between.

It did not take him long to learn of rules
– for those who did not remained fools –
there was no gold in sweat of brow
or walking straight behind a plow.
It was in the buying of things with gold
which someone else dug or stole.

Happy Jack cared not for labor
stealing pokes or sharpening sabers.
He made his nut by selling moose,
caribou, salmon, grouse and goose
in the round or striped and dried
or in bulk those who fried

the meat in pans with wine
and served it on planks of pine.
He took his pay in nuggets only
and hid them on the tundra daily
for just as the stampeders had come
they would leave with every crumb.

Happy Jack could see the truth
and could foretell every tooth
on the shore of the Norton Sound
would be south homeward bound
and he would have to leave the town
or his path would be *barabara* bound.

The northland is an unforgiving spouse
and life is more than just a sturdy house,
and patching every crack and chink
it means stocking homes with food and drink
for the Alaskan year to one's dismay
has but three months and all start with J.

Happy Jack endured the Bonfire Saloon
For it was his makeshift barracoon
to see if it were true he could live like these fools
who squandered every dollar and then cried pule
and leave the north as they had come
with empty pokes and reek of rum.

Maggie the Bag

"You got it right, I'm Maggie the bag,
with a face like the bottom of a burlap bag.
I'm fat and I'm slow with bowling pin legs,
hair like a hog and face like a pig.
I'm the best you can find for a quarter a throw,
onesies or twosies or three in a row.

It's ever so easy to call me a hag
but in one evening I make gold in a bag.
While you miners spend days with gold pans to scour
gravel stream bottoms to make what I do in an hour.
Yeah, I'm a whore with bed burns on my back
and when I leave with your money I never look back.

Don't chuckle with humor! You men made me this way,
all women, that is, for every hour of every day
you treat us like brood hens producing eggs
our worth depending what's between the legs
of the children we spawn. Then the men go to work
leaving the girls to be judged by the children the birth."

Montana Pete

In the argot of the West,
beyond the Mississippi's breast
where cattle, snake and scorpion thrive
and men earn their pay on cattle drives
men like Montana Pete were clear-cut
and low as snakes in wagon ruts.

"Scum of the earth" was his fame.
And you could always find his name
on posters on post office walls
and in law and order halls
with a price upon his head
wanted: alive or dead.

A lickspittle of the lowest sort,
with the criminal element he did cavort
along remote wagon trails
and locomotive rails
where with gun and handkerchief
and dodged the noose and legal script.

One by one his companions fell
most to buckshot and all to hell
leaving Pete to often marvel
why he was not in the orchard marble
and so to avoid a frontier noose
he thought it best to vamoose.

He changed his name as those of his ilt
in the hope it would disguise his guilt
and took a steamship to the north
with what little he had in worth,
less than one hundred coins in hand
for this twenty years of brigand.

As long as no one knew his fame
no cop would find his name
on a steamship manifest
where he hid in tie and vest,
clothing to disguise his flight
when he boarded late one night.

There is a saying true as nails
that good returns on twin rails
like a train with boxcars loaded
giving back more than one promoted.
Evil comes back around as well
and with it come the hounds of hell.

Those who choose to commit crimes
to enrich their lives porcine
find it hard to leap off the carousel
and ride they will until the death bell
arrives at their door in blue outfit
with paper, ink and legal writ.

Montana Pete failed to keep
his pledge to stay off the street
and find a job and make a life
– perhaps with a shapely wife –
but found that honest labor stinks
and keeps one on penury's brink.

So after months of washing dishes,
slopping dogs and filleting fishes
he had enough of honest labor
and chose to again pick up the saber,
pistol and rapid steed
and once again do evil deeds.

To commit evil he did not hesitate
but in the North there's special fate
for those who want to rob and run
or spend their lucre on illicit fun,
there was but one way to leave the town
and come December all ships were gone.

Thus it was while sipping beer
Marshal Jew Bob with glasses clear
confronted Pete in the gloom
of the celebrating Bonfire Saloon
and stated with a voice quite low
it was time for Montana to go.

Marshal said, a telegram from the West
– and he had a copy in his vest –
that come the spring a writ would arrive
to find him where're he chose to hide
for murder, so Jew Bob said to Pete
it might be best if he beat feet.

Odd it was that when the snow comes down
when all telegraph lines were down
but this was unknown to Montana Pete
who it is said indeed did beat feet
and where he went sinks no man's star
as long as it is from Nome quite far.

Peg Legged Jack

Peg Legged Jack had been lost at sea,
that was what the telegram said,
which was odd since he
was far from being dead.
He could be found most winter nights
in the Bonfire Saloon
where he told wild tales of pirate fights
and the quest for gold doubloons.
In summer time he mined the beach
and when ice came he remained
as muscle in the breech
of the front door of the Bonfire bar

where he kept the derelicts out
in front he was a blackguard,
"Hey! Just let 'em shout."

"Kiss my go-to-Hell" he'd say,
a statement from the decks
of ships he'd been on too many days
and survived too many wrecks.
But there was one thing he knew true
no matter where you trundle
it's the gold you take with you
even loaded to the gunnels.
He could make an eagle squeal
and banked his gold and script.
He did not drink to keep an even keel
as if he was still the captain of a ship.
"I've spent my life on many boats
Now all I want's a pine overcoat."

Economic Willie

Economic Willie was always chilly
    but what can you expect from a Mex
who was born in a shed on a Mazatlán bed
    before going to a med school in the sticks?
Brown as a bean and amazing lean,
    he was a bonafide doc
who also healed dogs, cattle and hogs
    and charged for his service bedrock.

With his wife and son, and plenty of rum,
    to sooth the extraction of teeth
his hours were long for there was a throng
    who preferred him to a wreath.
Be it bones broken from socks or the French Pox
    jaundice, cancer or rash
Economic Willie was often willing
    to take promise in lieu of cash.

He'd taken a test with the best of the rest
    and received his citizen's papers.
With no accent it seemed he was the American dream
    and he rose from the ranks of the paupers.
In Mexican clines there was no way to climb
    out of the rank of your birth
but north of the border there was no set order
    and all rewards came from your work.

This northern sawbones had no bones
    sledding into the bush to aid
the unfortunate many who had not a penny
    to pay for the services made.
Every evening and noon at the Bonfire Saloon
    he would pass the hat for the poor
and everyone gave for if they were ever grave-
    -ly ill he would not show them the door.

The doc was a card with a joke or canard
　　for humor's the best potion for ills
for those can't laugh are their own epitaph
　　for a chuckle's as good as a pill.
He was famous to say that an apple a day
　　will keep the doctor away,
then he added a quip as a post script
　　"But it will depend on your aim."

In his waiting room was a skeleton whom
　　he had purchased for medical school.
It hung on a wire and often did spiral
　　and was used as a medicinal tool.
Should a parent stall 'till a child's face was palled,
　　the doc had a tale to relate.
He'd point at the bones and say in low tones,
　　"He also came to me late."

Once a patent complained of two places of pain
　　and the doc replied with a snore,
"If you've come to complain of two places with pain
　　don't go back there anymore."
His favorite tale was one of a quail
　　whose husband had chocked on a carrot
so she bought a headstone which, standing alone,
　　had the weight of ten carats.

STEVE LEVI

As a writer of both fiction and nonfiction, Steve Levi's motto is simple: "If you do not have something unique, you have nothing." The literary world does not need another book on Alexander Hamilton or a drunk, disgraced, detective going through a divorce who is suddenly rehired by the police department for the 'biggest case in his/her career." Courtesy of the internet, America is entering a Golden Age of Literature. A decade ago, the New York publishers did not publish good books. They published books they gambled would sell in bookstores. Today, bookstores are gone. Now readers can find books on any subject online. Books, particularly fiction, do not have to be genre to sell; they just have to be good.

A good example of breaking out of the cement of genres are Steve Levi's "impossible crime" mysteries. An impossible crime is one where the detectives must solve HOW the crime was committed before he/she can go after the perpetrators. In *The Matter of the Vanishing Greyhound*, for example, four robbers leave a bank in San Francisco with a dozen hostages,

$10 million in cash and the contents of all of the safety deposit boxes. They demand a Greyhound bus in which to escape. With the police following, the criminals vanish after they drive out onto the Golden Gate Bridge. Before the detective can apprehend the perpetrators he has to find them. And if the bandits already have the money, why do they need the hostages? Steve Levi's impossible crime novels can be found at www.authormasterminds.com/steve-levi.

If you prefer nonfiction, there are Levi's books on the Alaska Gold Rush. So little is known of the Alaska Gold Rush most people believe the Klondike Rush – made famous by Robert Service and Jack London – *IS* the Alaska Gold Rush. Not so. The Klondike Gold Rush was centered in Dawson in the Yukon Territory of Canada. It only lasted about 14 months. The Alaska Gold Rush lasted from 1880 to the Second World War, and covered an area 1/5 the size of the lower 48 states. The Alaska Gold Rush has been an untapped mine of fascinating events, interesting people, unique places and untold stories – until now!

In addition to the illustrations in this book, other historic photographs of Nome can be found at https://vilda.alaska.edu. VILDA is the acronym for the Visual Library of Digital Alaskana. Artwork was by Amanda Saxton.

Law and order in Alaska during the Gold Rush was disjointed. The Governor was appointed by the President of the United States but was within the Department of the Interior. Judges were in the Justice Department but only in Juneau, Nome, and Fairbanks. In other communities, some magistrates acted as judges and, in smaller communities, miners' councils whose membership was composed of who was there at the time of the trial. Offshore, law and order was the jurisdiction of the Revenue Cutter Service, seen here. In 1915, the Revenue Cutter Service and the Lifesaving Service were consolidated into the United States Coast Guard.